**TAKE ACTION
WITH ANIMALS!**

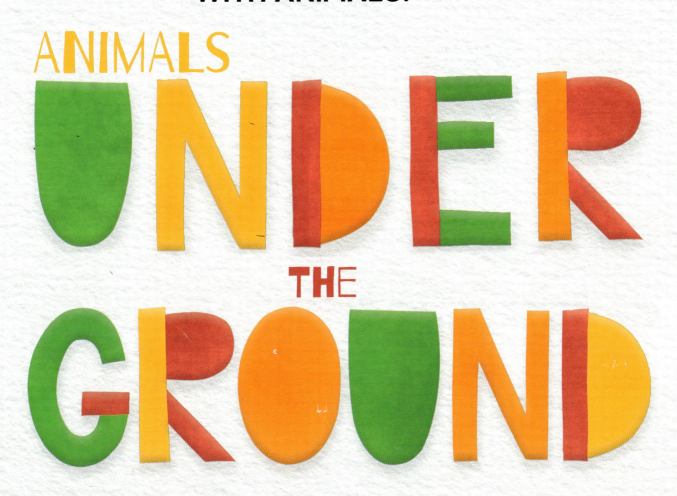

ANIMALS UNDER THE GROUND

Written by
Madeline Tyler

Illustrated by
Amy Li

Published in 2022 by Windmill Books,
an Imprint of Rosen Publishing
29 East 21st Street, New York, NY 10010

Edited by: John Wood
Illustrated by: Amy Li

Cataloging-in-Publication Data

Names: Tyler, Madeline. | Li, Amy.
Title: Animals under the ground / by Madeline Tyler, illustrated by Amy Li.
Description: New York : Windmill Books, 2022. | Series: Take action with animals!
Identifiers: ISBN 9781499487466 (pbk.) | ISBN 9781499487480 (library bound) | ISBN 9781499487473 (6 pack) | ISBN 9781499487497 (ebook)
Subjects: LCSH: Burrowing animals--Juvenile fiction. | Underground areas--Juvenile fiction.
Classification: LCC PZ7.1.T954 An 2022 | DDC [E]--dc23

Printed in the United States of America

CPSIA Compliance Information: Batch CSWM22: For Further Information contact Rosen
Publishing, New York, New York at 1-800-237-9932

Find us on

All images courtesy of Shutterstock. With thanks to Getty Images, Thinkstock Photo and iStockphoto.

Cover – KateChe, arigato, AlexZaitev, L.Kramer, EV-DA, flovie, Toluk. Recurring backgrounds – YamabikaY. Recurring font – KateChe. Recurring
texture brushes – Toluk (grunge), flovie (spotty), aksenova_yu (grass). 2–3 – AlexZaitev, 4–7 – Grinbox, 8–11 – freesoulproduction, Nadya_Art,
Grinbox, 12–15 – AlexZaitevm arigato, VectorShow, 16–19 – L.Kramer, EV-DA, Karbo_Kreto, Mascha Tace, 20–23 – Lorelyn Medina.

Can you use your imagination
to take a trip underground?

Follow the

INSTRUCTIONS

on each page and see what you can find.

Rabbits can jump a very long way.

Can you gently

the rabbit's nose to make it jump?

Off it hops!

Bye-bye, rabbit!

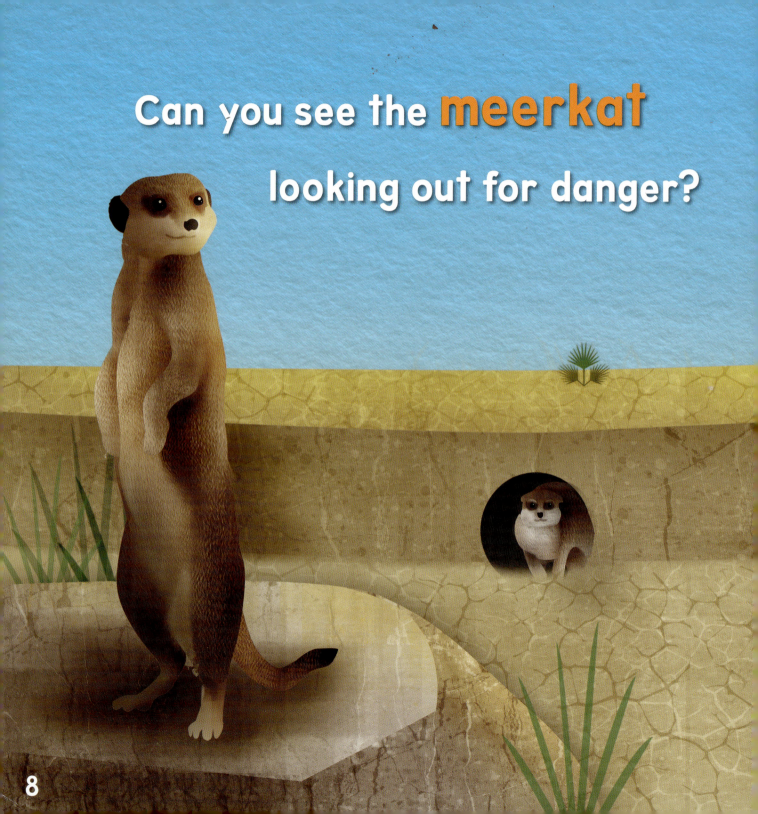

Can you see the **meerkat** looking out for danger?

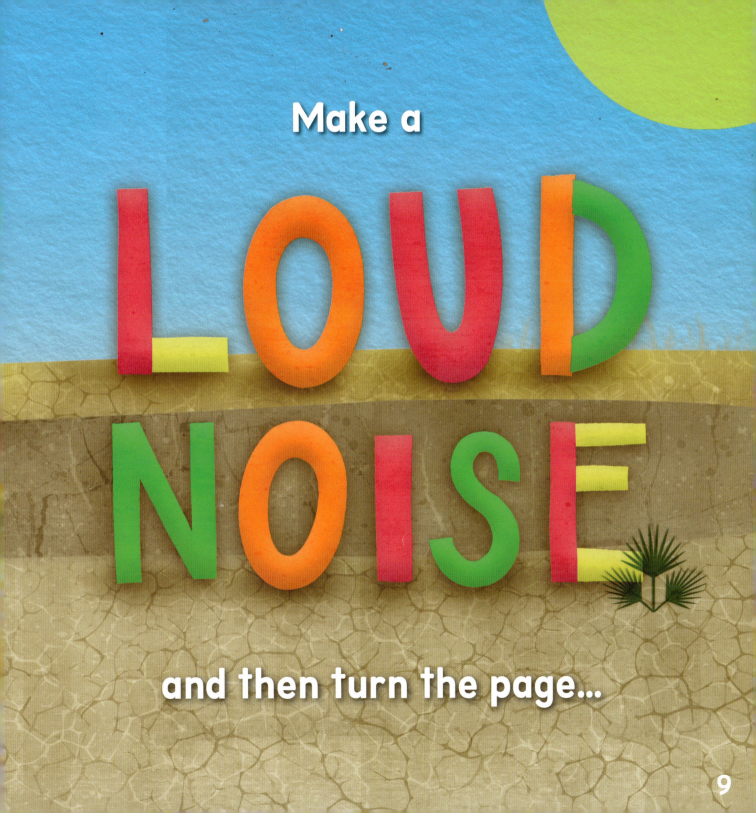

Make a

LOUD NOISE

and then turn the page...

All the meerkats
have come out to play!

Can you count them all?

Where are all the **worms?**

Pretend your fingers are raindrops and

TAP

the page.

Tap, tap, tap...

The worms have come up to say
hello!

Look, an
armadillo!

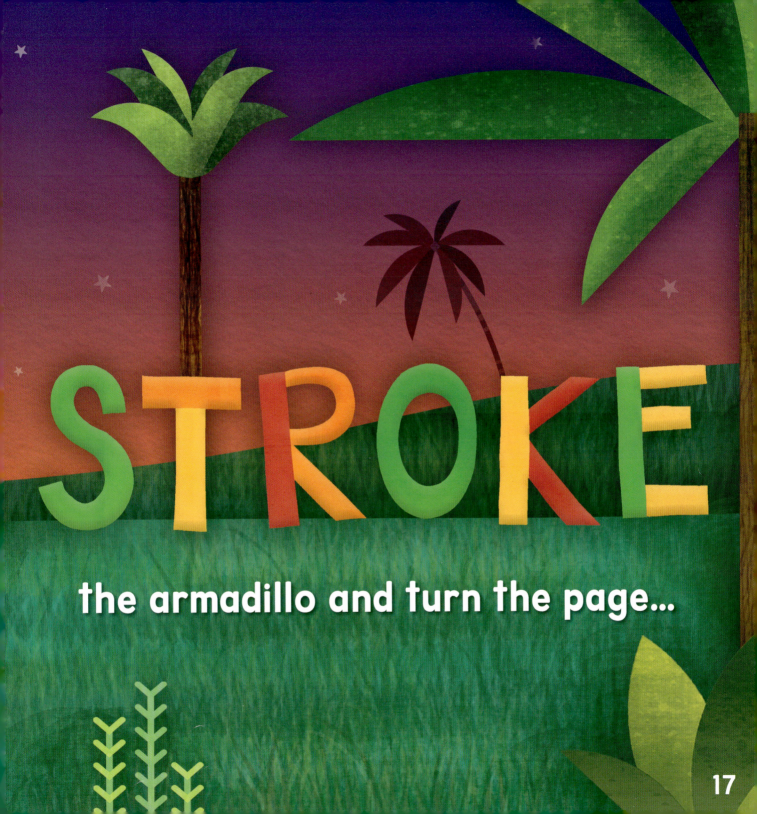

STROKE

the armadillo and turn the page...

The armadillo has rolled
up into a ball!

Porcupines have lots of spiky hair called quills.

What will happen if you

SHAKE

this book and then turn the page?

Look!

Now its quills are all standing up!

Can you tell what belongs to which animal?